TCC South

Crowley Learning Center

MAKING the JUMP >>>

MAKING *the* >>> JUMP

How to Successfully Transition from High School to College

Rochelle Moore, Ed.S.

ClearVision Publishing

Nashville, Tennessee

First Edition

Library of Congress Catalog Publication Data
ISBN: 978-0-692-47892-9

Published by ClearVision Publishing, Nashville, TN

Design and layout by MyDpiDesign

Edited by Seven Hills Communications and the Xlibris Corporation

Printed in the United States of America

To my children—Jasmine, Isaiah, and Caleb—who encouraged me to share my passion. To my loving husband who always encourages me. To my mentor, Dr. Virlyn Williams, for her constant guidance, and to all the individuals who inspired and motivated me to write.

Contents

Introduction

During my high school years, I only focused on graduating and looking forward to the day I could sleep in as opposed to getting up for another first day of high school. Nowhere in my scenario was college an option, and since college was not in my plans, I had not properly prepared myself for college.

The American College Test (ACT) or the Scholastic Aptitude Test (SAT) was not taken as recommended prior to graduation, nor were applications filled out to begin the college registration process. My guidance counselor, Mrs. Camellia Gregory, would periodically pull me to the side and ask, "Which standardized test have you taken?" or "Which college or university are you interested in enrolling?"

My answer to Ms. Gregory was always simple and to the point: "I am not going to college. I am going to airline school. I want to be an airline stewardess."

After spending my entire life in school, committing to another four years (at the time) seemed senseless. So I leaned toward airline school. I chose airline school because the program was quick, and I figured that I could quickly begin making money.

After graduating from high school, I continued to work and pursued airline school. Before going into class for the training, there were modules and tests that I had to complete. After a number of the modules and tests were completed, training began.

I remember it as if it were yesterday. It was a cold September when I began my training, but the days seemed even colder because the school was miles away in another state, far from the warmth of my family that I had become accustomed to. Though I felt wintery on the inside and out, I eventually completed all the module and testing requirements along with the in-class training to begin my career as an airline stewardess!

I was on my way—at least that's what I thought. That autumn of that same year, I became pregnant. That was the point where I realized that I needed to refocus my plans because I wanted a career that would allow me an opportunity to be with my new child. So, the question shifted from, "How do I put myself in a position to make money?" to "What career will give me a better opportunity to spend time with my new child?"

Now, I'm sure many airline stewardesses successfully manage their jobs *and* are great parents at the same time, yet I knew that this situation would not work for me. The only thing I knew at the time was that a child was not in my scenario. I spent many days and nights rethinking traveling across the country, knowing that I would soon have a responsibility that can't be shuffled into my parents' laps. I had to rethink my whole career choice because life was becoming very real really fast.

After graduating from airline school, I pursued employment with airline companies. Now, despite worrying about becoming a new mother with a new job that would keep me miles from my new infant, I was not able to land a job with an airline company because I was considered too short. Really . . . height challenged!

I could not believe it. All I wanted to do after graduating from high school was become an airline stewardess, and it now appeared that that would never happen. Despite all the challenges I brought to the table, it appeared that my hopes and dreams were flying away. Even worse, that was my only plan after graduating from high school. I needed a way to care for my unborn child, and I quickly realized the minimum wage job that I had currently had would not support me and a child. I needed a career. If only I had paid a little more attention to Ms. Gregory. *What did she say I needed to do?*

I remembered that she always said that college was a pathway that led to many careers. So I came home and prepared to enroll into college. But, as previously mentioned, I had not taken the ACT or the SAT—nor had I applied for any colleges. So I studied for the ACT and took the test to gain college entrance.

Soon after, I applied to a university in my area. Now this preparation and new yearning to enter college came after learning that I was with child. Honestly, I was not ready for the transition into motherhood, nor was I mentally prepared for college. Because I planned much later to transition into college, I was ill prepared for having what it took to become successful on the next level.

Although I was admitted into a university, remedial courses were needed to strengthen my core competencies. Remedial courses are developmental classes that students are required to take to help them succeed on a college level. The purpose for the remedial courses is for students to develop basic academic skills to be successful in their university courses (Long, 2009). Being more prepared is good; however, the problem is that remedial classes do not count toward a student's program of study. In other words, for each remedial class one takes, no course credit is received.

According to Adams (2010), "college-readiness benchmarks were developed by ACT to predict whether a student has a 75 percent chance of earning a C or higher or a 50 percent chance of earning a B or higher in a usual first-year college course." Typically, students who do not score high on their ACT or SAT standardized test must take remedial courses. Not only did it feel like I was wasting time taking remedial classes that did not count, but I also had a hard time because I really did not have a clear vision, any expectations, or goals to guide me through. All I knew was to go to college in hopes of finding a way to care for my future child.

My story is only one of the millions of stories of students who struggle during the transition from high school to college. But like me, do not get caught in an alarming transition.

Take full advantage of this book! The purpose for writing *Making the Jump: How to Successfully Transition from High School to College* is to inform rising juniors, graduating high school seniors, and incoming freshmen (especially first-generation college students) of the importance of preparing to transition from high school to college successfully. The truth is, according to Christopher Gearon (2015), "fully one-third of [college] freshmen don't return for [their] sophomore year."

If you are reading this book, you have begun a process that will bring clarity to you in areas where others will, unfortunately, stumble.

This book is created to help students become more informed of postsecondary educational expectations, such as how to harness your vision, how to set expectations beyond your comfort zones, the importance of creating goals, and how to attack them. You will also learn what it means to be independently responsible as well as key coping skills required to set healthy boundaries. In addition to these key points, there are many other principles that this book will introduce to you, which are designed to make your transition from high school to college as smooth as possible.

It is important that you understand the demands that university courses and college life will bring you. According to *Beyond the Rhetoric* (2010), every year in the United States, nearly 60 percent of first-year college students discover that, despite being fully eligible to attend college, they are not academically ready for postsecondary studies. Transitioning from high school to an institution without the proper teaching, learning, and experience allows one to recognize that he or she has a lot to learn.

In essence, college readiness requires preparation. During high school, preparation for postsecondary education should be strictly enforced to ensure college readiness. When it came to interest, knowledge, and test preparation, I failed myself—which made my transitional years very difficult. But that was me.

There is only one question that matters: "How ready are you?"

1

Vision

According to Dictionary.com, vision is described as picturing something in the mind or envisioning the future now. Let's say that a vacation is long overdue and it's time to get away, so you go and fill up your car with gas. You see, it's not enough to know that you want to get away. You have to know where you're going so that you can plan accordingly. Unfortunately, a full tank of gas is not sufficient to get you from wherever you are to an appointed destination.

After filling up your car with anticipation of going on vacation, what good is it to just get in the car and go? You need to know how far to go, how much money to bring, how much time the trip will take, and most importantly, you will need to know which direction to take. Without vision, one lacks direction; and without direction, it's almost impossible to reach a desired destination. You don't have to believe me; even the Good Book says that people without vision perish.[1] Simply put, a vision connects what *is* to what *can be*. So where are you headed? This question especially applies to college students.

For students to be successful in college, he or she has to know where he or she sees themselves after graduation. A lot of students do not succeed simply because they fail to see themselves walking their vision (of themselves) out.

---

[1] Proverbs 29:18 (KJV)

When I entered the state university, I had no idea what I would be doing after graduation. I did understand that taking classes for a program of study would allow completion and a degree. Yet if I had known which profession I wanted as a career after graduation, I would have made better academic decisions along the way.

For example, I would not have chosen nursing as my initial program of study if I knew I was more inclined to helping develop a person's mind as opposed to being an advocate for the care of individuals. In addition, the program of nursing required an extensive amount of reading and note-taking in classes that nullified me. This is not to suggest that other programs do not require the same thing, but it is important to dive into a program that provides courses and material that will stimulate each student's mind.

To illustrate, think on this example: it's foolish to plan a trip to the Mardi Gras with all the bright lights and colorful parades if what you seek is a peaceful and relaxing vacation. You have to vision yourself in a program that aligns with your core self. In other words, from the beginning, envision what excites you. Seeing yourself as what you envision will help you take the right direction.

Visioning yourself now as what you want to become tomorrow is an important tool to use while transitioning from high school to college. Therefore, how do you see yourself after graduation? Does the university that you are interested in have a program that will get you to your career destination?

Students who have an idea in mind of where they're headed understand that somewhere along the way during the college experience, certain classes must be taken to support their vision. I lacked this direction coming from high school to college. I had no idea. And guess what? It's not just me.

What if you don't have a vision of what you want to become after graduation? There are two steps that can be applied in this situation: (1) dream and (2) create a personal academic vision statement.

Now is as good of a time as ever to learn to dream. When you walk into a room, do people speak of you as they did Joseph? Do they say "here comes that dreamer?"[2] Learn to dream BIG.

I have two teenage sons who both want to become doctors. Sure, this may change as they get a little older, but the point is that their future dreams have given them direction. As teenagers, they understand that to become a neurosurgeon and a pulmonologist, there is a certain level of math classes, STEM[3] summer programs, extracurricular activities, and certain types of community service projects that must be acquired to be accepted into the college that can

---

[2] Genesis 37:19 (NIV)
[3] Science, technology, engineering, and mathematics

further their journeys on their roads that lead to their visions. No matter your age, envision yourself as a victor in some fashion and walk that way.

Another notion that students need to know is what will work for them. This is where a personal academic vision statement will help. Having success in college includes being aware of what one likes and dislikes in a college or university. For example, is he or she comfortable with a large university? Or would they do better in a small community-type institution?

"The typical small college is a school that has an enrollment of less than 5,000 students, doesn't have a graduate school, and has a student-to-faculty ratio of less than 10:1—some are even as low as 5:1" (Hyman and Jacobs, 2010).

When I enrolled into the state university, enrollment or class sizes were not what I considered at all. I had not prepared for what would be a good fit for me. All I knew was to go to college.

You can avoid this by simply knowing what works best for you. This way, you avoid getting caught up in trying to go to a big-named school, hoping that it's a good fit for you.

College success is dependent on students who aspire to achieve. Students must have a desire, hope, and a longing for academic success. These attributes don't begin in college; they begin in middle and high school. Students who have "winner" traits yearn to be victorious and are always willing to do what it takes to become successful. This suggests going to class, doing homework, studying, reading ahead, and visiting professors for better understanding even when you don't feel like it.

Is this you? Believe me, students who do more than what is required or recommended will have college success. Students who aspire to do more will accomplish more, and students who walk toward their personal vision will achieve college success. Walking toward your vision is the beginning of success, but how do you take the first step? You must spend time writing out a *scholastic vision statement.*

According to Covey (1989), "a statement will change you because it forces you to think through your priorities deeply, carefully, and to align your behavior with your belief." He goes on to say that "a statement is not something you write overnight. It takes deep introspection, careful analysis, thoughtful expression, and often many rewrites to produce it in final form."

Here are the steps to writing a fulfilling vision statement.

Writing a scholastic vision statement:

1. Write a scholastic vision statement for yourself. Make sure that your vision statement aligns with passions, your core values, and your aspirations:

a. What are your passions?

b. What are your core values?

c. What are your aspirations?

d. Where are you headed?

e. Make it clear and visible.

f. Think big.

g. Time: make sure it's at least five years out.

2. Keep a copy on you at all times, and keep a copy on your mirror so that it's a reminder to yourself that you are headed somewhere. The description of these two copies, if read enough, will eventfully become words inscribed onto your heart. The goal is through this process your vision will eventfully spill out of your heart which overtime will drive your attitude and passion.

In Other Words

When I was in high school, I knew someday that I would become a dentist. That vision consciously or subconsciously guided me to do my best in school and stay out of trouble.

—*Yonathan Nigatu,*
Meharry Medical College

If you don't have a vision, then you're really clueless to why you are even in school.

—*Terry Bean,*
Western Kentucky University

Relating my major to a vision was not important to me as a freshman, but as time went on, having a vision was key to ensuring that I was on track to completing my degree.

—*Marsha Thompson,*
Tennessee State University

2
Goals

It is always good to start whatever you do with the end in mind. So as you see yourself walking across the stage receiving a diploma, what type of graduate will you become? Will you be in the top percent of your class? Will you be one who led college organizations? Will you distinguish yourself as a community service leader? Will you conduct undergraduate research? Will you gain experience through internships?

There are so many questions that can be posed. The point is to think now of what you'll need to make your transition as smooth as possible after you graduate with your undergraduate degree. In other words, know where you want to end up well before you get started.

In the previous chapter, you created a scholastic vision statement, which is great because it provides direction. Now we must create clear goals that will help your vision become an active reality.

Most of the time, students have an idea of where they want to go but miss key opportunities to make tactful moves that advance them toward their desired destination. In today's competitive world, it's no secret that students must excel in as many areas as possible to stand out. So create goals now that will help you to market yourself as a high-achieving academic scholar as well as a student that participated in activities and organizations.

To become a top scholar, you must learn to attack your studies with ambition, determination, and persistence. Because you are reading this book, I'm guessing that you are a motivated person. If so, great, because motivation is a quality that you must have to reach part A of your end goal—become a top scholar.

After high school graduation, students who are aware of their end goal and possess motivation are more likely to find success. Knowing where you want to end up is fine, but you must create a detailed plan. Yes, the first, second, third, and succeeding steps must be identified. Being truthful, this was an area in which I had to learn the hard way.

When I enrolled into the state university, I did not have goals. Regrettably, having no plan prolonged my stay at the university. I started out in a nursing program but graduated in psychology. Thankfully, many courses transferred over, but if I had a plan previously, it would have saved me the time and money. Please, don't take my route.

Plan before you begin. Align your goals with your vision. Create for yourself a road map. It is important to have a target for what you are attempting to accomplish. What does one hope to achieve from choosing a particular institution or program of study? What is the point? When students recognize what their goal is before enrolling into a university, it keeps them focused.

It is important for students not only to have a goal in mind but a plan and a purpose. Entertain aligning your goals with your vision. So do not plan to attend a university without setting goals. I can't say it enough, but be smart, create goals, and stay motivated to ensure you receive a high grade point average (GPA) that represents your passion. Use your goals and motivation to create a scholastic legacy for yourself.

The second part (part B) of marketing yourself for a strong future is to make sure that you participate in activities that will promote you as a serious candidate for whichever direction your objectives point you toward. Besides being scholastic, make sure that your goals speak to the fact that you are an exceptionally engaged and active student as well.

For instance, maximize your college experience by interning at an organization or business. This will give you an opportunity to apply textbook principles in a real-world environment. Maybe you can create a goal to become active in your community. For example, manage a blood drive, feed the homeless, or tutor at a local community center.

Next, there are also many student organizations that you could join. Joining student organizations gives one an opportunity to enhance leadership qualities. These activities are important to include as you set goals that lead to your ultimate scholastic vision because they teach you qualities that a textbook just cannot teach. Being active in organizations will teach you how to build partnerships through collaboration, how to manage conflict, how to lead, and how to train others to lead or serve.[4] Make sure you become active; it's one of the best ways to have no doubt that you will become a well-rounded individual.

As you set your goals, do not hesitate to be ambitious, determined, and persistent. Students who incorporate these qualities into their goal setting will have a good chance of making their scholastic vision statement become a reality.

---

[4] *Transforming a College: A Story of a Little-Known College's Strategic Climb to National Distinction*. George Keller. Baltimore, MD: John Hopkins University Press, 2004. p. 51

To give you a better idea of what type of credentials you should pursue, a sample resume of a pre-med student aiming to become very desirable after college is provided on the next page.

John Hillman

<u>Community Service</u>

Temple Foreign Missions—Belize

Dental work for underserved, 2014

Nashville Rescue Mission

Tutored GED students, 2014–2015

<u>Education</u>

Fisk University, class of 2017, **GPA 3.8**

Premedical Club,

Member, 2012–2015, president, 2016

<u>Employment</u>

Dialysis Center Inc. (internship)

Assisted in outpatient coordination of

transplants, 2016

Southern Community Cohort Study

Collaboration with Meharry Medical

College, researched lung, prostate, and

breast cancer, 2015

THRUST Math and Science Program

Counselor, summer units, 2012–2013

<u>Athletic Achievements</u>

Men's Cross Country, 2012

In Other Words

Goal writing is a lost art; it should really be taught in high school.

—*Dr. Avery Finch*,
Trevecca Nazarene University

There will come a time in college when things become too stressful. Times like this are overcome by being goal oriented. Yes, the process might hinder spontaneous activities with friends, but the benefits far outweigh the negative.

—*Yonathan Nigatu*,
Meharry Medical College

Remember this, without goals you are more vulnerable to negative influences.

—*Michael Harris*,
Jackson State University

3

Time Management

The key to time management is simple . . .
value every moment.

—*Menachem Schneerson*

Let me give you a fair warning: in college, procrastination *is* the culprit. Fortunately for me, this was an area in which I was actually adequate. I have always possessed an ability to manage time. Nevertheless, what is time management?

According to *Wikipedia*, time management is the act or process of planning and exercising conscious control over the amount of time spent on specific activities, especially to increase effectiveness, efficiency, or productivity.[5]

---

[5] http://en.wikipedia.org/wiki/Time_management

Let's be honest. Having this quality speaks volumes, and frankly, it goes without saying, but if success is the ultimate goal, to lack this ability puts one at a serious disadvantage. Individuals who are able to prioritize their days simply complete more tasks. No matter the task, prioritizing and completing tasks will help you get it done, and this is an essential tool needed to be successful in college.

In college, there are a number of social events, assignments, and activities that will all vie to top your priority list. The freedom you will have will cause you to lose sight of what is important and what is not. Oftentimes, you will have to choose the harder choice. Do I study late, or do I go to the party? Do I go to the gym, or do I go back to bed? Do I go to the business club meeting, or do I go to the library?

Choosing to prioritize tasks will help you avoid time-management conflicts. There is no way around it. If you plan to have success in college, you must use your time wisely. Because there will be so much pulling for your time, you must get ahead of this potential issue by planning to control how you spend your days. Give yourself an advantage; make time management an asset. Trust me, many of your peers will not posses this quality entering college, and if you are able to manage time effectively, you will separate yourself from the pack simply because you understand the importance of putting things in order and creating a schedule.

No matter which college graduate you ask, just about all of them have memories of having fun. There are some events students just will not miss. It's no secret—college social events are very important. I know most college professors, academic advisors, and so on would tell you that assignments are most important (and they are); however, social activities will fight the most to throw off your priorities. Therefore, as we begin to put together a schedule, we are going to go ahead and list a social event that you want to attend each week. Yes, look at your calendar, and go ahead and pencil in that fraternity party or that music festival that you want to attend. This way, you will go ahead and get the conflict out of the way. If there is no conflict with what else needs your attention for the week—such as studying, going to see your professor, exercising, etc.—you are more likely to stick with everything else you've planned to do.

As long as you know when you're going to have some fun during the week, it becomes easier to prioritize everything else that ensures your success. So I'll go against conventional wisdom here. My advice is to plan one social event that you want to attend first. This way, there are no excuses for doing everything else you need to do to manage your time efficiently.

The next item on the agenda is to ensure that assignments and study times are added to your daily routine. Carving out study time is necessary for college success. Studying doubles once students are enrolled into college (*Surviving College*, 2014).

Students who attend a university have so much to manage. Each class will have its own demands, but they are easily managed if you know what you need to do well in advance.

Do have a plan to study well in advance? If you have a test coming up, when is it? This system will allow you to *not* have to cram at the last minute. Do you need to do some reading? If so, how many chapters before your obligations are due? Based on that, how many pages should you read each day? Also, where will you study? Sometimes the library is more suitable. Sometimes it's best to learn in a study group. You may need to visit your professor with questions you have during his or her office hours, or maybe you can just study in your room.

No matter where you decide to study, read, or do homework assignments, each week, you must plan a specific time to do all things required for each class that you have. You can itemize these events by using a time-management clock or by using a daily task list (we'll discuss these tools at the end of this chapter).

Students should take classes according to other responsibilities in their lives in order for study time to be effective. Students have to remember, along with other requirements, that study time is essential.

According to *Surviving College* (2014), "for every one credit hour in which students enroll, he or she will spend approximately two to three hours outside of class studying. Therefore, to help determine the course load most appropriate, use the formula: 12 credit hours (4 courses) = 12 hours in class per week = 24 to 36 hours study time per week."

Setting aside time daily to prepare for class is mandatory if you want to excel academically. Carve out time in your schedule to ensure that you succeed.

In addition to making sure you add a social event and carving out time to do assignments, you also need to make sure that you allot time for extracurricular activities. These are activities such as track and field, golf, marching band, concert choir, a pre-nursing club, the psychology club, or the forensic team. These clubs and organizations are very important because leadership and character are both developed during these activities.

University clubs also assist students in their academic success because they help them learn to prioritize. Students who participate in extracurricular activities are more likely to demonstrate time-management skills (Rivers, 2014).

Extracurricular activities can be demanding of your time. So as you create your schedule, it is imperative that you make sure that you add these activities to time slots that do not conflict with your study times. Students who do not manage their time will begin to lose focus as to what matters most and will quickly fall into the trap of overlapping. According to Rivers (2014), "students who participate in extracurricular activities are more likely to feel confident in their ability to multitask."

So as you entertain a social life, work hard to maintain good grades, and participate in extracurricular activities, remember that time management will help you balance all areas of your life. In other words, take control of your time. There are so many things that require a student's time, such as exercising or even working a job. Just make sure that you take control of your time by providing structure.

No matter what part of the world you live in or which university you attend, there are seven days in every week and twenty-four hours in each day. Think about it, all the great people that we know took full advantage of their twenty-four hours a day. Thus, the same must be true for us; there is no time to waste.

Do not lose sight of time by procrastinating, slacking, or being slothful. Use your time wisely and create opportunities to work toward greater success. Use time management as a tool to succeed in college. Let time management help you govern and maintain self-discipline over social opportunities, study time, and extracurricular activities.

We must take control of every minute of our lives. If not, we'll get caught saying "if only I had more time." However, here's a point to remember. Oprah, Mother Teresa, Neil Tyson, Thurgood Marshall, Albert Einstein, Nelson Mandela, Gandhi, and Martin Luther King all had the same twenty-four hours as we do. So let's also take full advantage of every moment.

College will pull you from each direction all at the same time. Actually, college is the perfect place to learn how to manage time. Do not be mistaken. Students that equip themselves with time management as a tool will prepare themselves for college success and beyond.

- Time-Management Clock
    - Create alarms for yourself:
        - Who doesn't have a calendar on their phone these days?
        - Alarms could alert you of upcoming assignment deadlines, etc.

- Daily Task List
  - Pen, paper—simply write it down[6]
    - First, add a social event that you plan on attending
    - Next add your classes, adequate study time, which aligns with the amount of class hours that you have
    - Add assignment and test deadlines
    - Add extracurricular activities (university organizations, sport teams, etc.)
    - Finally, add hobbies (exercising, swimming, etc.)

---

[6] The Good Book says to write it down and make it plain (Habakkuk 2:2).

In Other Words

Balance school work and fun time with good time management skills. Set a time in place for doing what you need to do and what you want to do.

—*Frederick Cartwright Jr.*, Fisk University

If you are not goal oriented, it's very unlikely that you will graduate.

—*Elijah D. Holt*, Tennessee State University

Don't stumble through your first year. Create a routine and stick with it. Most likely your routine will change though, so be adjustable but stick with a plan.

—*Carlyle Edwards*, University of Tennessee Knoxville

Planning my time in advance helped me enjoy my free time. Time management is the biggest key for success in college.

—*Yonathan Nigatu*, Meharry Medical College

4

Coping Skills

It's already bad that you sleep on the top bunk of your dorm room of three, but what's even worse is that one of your roommates studies late. This means that you lie under a ceiling light that stares at you until 3:00 a.m. each morning! Now this has never been an issue, so you are really trying to figure out how to deal with this dilemma in a civil manner.

When entering higher education, you will need survival-skill tools to help you deal with difficult situations efficiently. This is essential to sustaining a healthy and balanced you. Each student's challenge may vary, but all will face many difficulties and obstacles along the way. How students react to those challenges is the true measurement of growth.

Because demands are intensified and will, at least, appear to occur more frequently once you enter college, it's a must that you adjust from the way you coped with challenges, stressors, and disappointments in high school. Despite these difficulties, there are tools that can help you manage while in college. Tools that you can acquire to help are reading, journaling, exercising, and conflict management. These are examples of skills needed to help you overcome or adapt to problems and situations that loom.

All entering college freshmen know that tests will come, yet many are unfamiliar with the challenges that await them. For example, it is no secret that college is significantly different and much harder than high school; nevertheless, each year, a new batch of incoming freshmen is baffled by the demands of college course requirements. Students must have adequate coping skills to combat the challenges that lie ahead, even beyond the classroom.

Making new social connections is a challenge for new students. It doesn't seem hard, but making new friends in college can be more complicated than one would think.

Do they abuse drugs and/or alcohol?

Will these new friends try to pressure me into having unwanted sex?

Though you may have worked through the answers to most of these questions in high school, trying to master the college social world can be a whole new beast.

Another challenge that can cause college students to stumble is trying to figure out how to handle newly found independence. Besides time management and managing money, managing one's own health can also be hard work for those who have never really had to take these matters seriously.

Even though these challenges seem like headaches at the time, they actually help young people become mature and respectable adults. So welcome your challenges. My only hope is that you are prepared to cope with them as you journey through your college years. As you learn coping skills, use them because how you utilize them determines the outcome of each challenge. Learn to adjust your emotions, thoughts, and behaviors to each challenge.

Learn to deal with disappointments. Yes, disappointments are a part of life, but when you are in high school, most people have lifelong friends and family for such times. Since college students are building new networks, disappointments can be more detrimental simply because you may not know who to turn to for support to discuss the many misfortunes that are sure to come.

In life, frustrations are inevitable. You will get bad reports, bad grades, and you will even not be chosen for the lead position that you know you are overqualified for. Yet all of that will be okay because in life, everything doesn't always turn out as we hope. So, students do not look at disappointments as failure but as a learning experience. Those of you who recognize where you went wrong are at a greater advantage because it is unlikely that you will allow disappointment to get an upper hand on you again on the same situation.

In other words, failing is okay as long as you learn from your mistakes. Use disappointments as life coaches. Students, disappointments will come, but learn to use them as stepping stones.

In high school, you would have never thought that a light staring at you until three in the morning could stress you enough to affect your ability to succeed. But truthfully, the stress of challenges and disappointments can be overwhelming. In addition, high stress is no good for college students because this usually indicates that concentration is low. In other words, stress can be an attention grabber. However, stress does not have to be victorious in your life.

There are clues that can help you succeed over stress—learn to pay attention to your body. Believe it or not, your body will alarm you when things seem to be getting too hectic, and these signs will help you keep your stress levels low.

For example, "When your stomach is tight, it can be a sign of 'loss of control'; when you have a stiff neck, it can be a signal of inflexibility; and when your shoulders are tense, you may be taking on too much" Strike (2014).

Learn to recognize the many feelings that cause conditions associated with stress.

Here are a few activities that you can incorporate into your life when you begin to notice that stress is trying to set in:

✓ **Read**—Reading is a healthy escape from the stresses of life. By opening a book, you allow yourself to be invited into a literary world that distracts you from your daily stressors. "Reading can even relax your body by lowering your heart rate and easing the tension in your muscles." A 2009 study at the University of Sussex found that reading can reduce stress by up to 68 percent.[7]

✓ **Journal**—Journaling is an effective stress-relief exercise that helps reduce anxiety and the amount of worrying too.[8] By writing events that previously happened, you can reflect on what happened and have time to think through a positive solution.

✓ **Exercise**—Exercising can help muscles use pent-up energy and is effective in releasing muscle

---

[7] Center for Spirituality and Healing and Charlson Meadows, 2015. http://www.takingcharge.csh.umn.edu/tips-change/reading-stress-relief

[8] Krisha McCoy. "Journal Your Way to Stress Relief." http://www.everydayhealth.com/longevity/journal-for-stress-relief.aspx

tension before it can result in muscle pain or spasms. Exercise can also help to reduce pent-up frustration. It can also help you take your mind off problems while working out or just walking.[9]

✓ **Conflict Management**—Resolving conflicts helps students maintain healthy relationships. Because college is communal, having an ability to recognize and respect differences is essential.

All too often, students are faced with unfamiliarity in their lives. How he or she responds or reacts will determine his or her success. Students who learn to face challenges, disappointments, and stressors with a positive attitude have already won half the battle. This is where the coping skills of life come into action.

Be aware, physically and mentally, of where you are in life. This way, you can proactively choose a coping skill that will help you defuse the negative power that challenges

---

[9] 2014. http://www.stress-management-for-peak-performance.com/exercise-reduces-stress.html

and disappointments try to bring your way. Instead, use these situations as stepping stones, and I promise that you'll be able to use your college experiences to motivate someone else on the power of using coping skills in the future.

In Other Words

In college, I dealt with stress by committing to a hobby; I also surrounded myself with positive people who brought me out of my stressful state.

—Theron Blair,
Middle Tennessee State University

Small times of meditation really worked for me.

—Antonio Marks,
Tennessee State University

Find one thing that you are good at and makes you happy. For me, I played the piano and organ at church and worked out; this helped with stress and got me away from focusing on school.

—Eric Fennell,
South Carolina State University

PART II

5

Self-Efficacy

In order for students to have college success, one *must* develop self-efficacy. But what exactly is self-efficiency? Self-efficiency is the ability to self-regulate and persist in the face of difficulty. In other words, students must have the capacity and willpower to complete tasks and reach goals. Hopefully, your parents and high school teachers have promoted independence in you.

Usually, most high school teachers and parents will stay on you to ensure that tasks are complete—not so in college. This is why it is so important while making the transition from high school to college that self-efficacy is established.

There will be times when a twenty-page paper is due and marching band practice doesn't end until 9:00 p.m. Guess what? Your paper is still due! It's not going to matter that you are tired, and it is not going to fly that homecoming events are vying for your time. You'll have to find it in yourself to complete the assignments on time!

It may seem weird, but you will have to become your own cheerleader. You will have to believe in yourself when no one else does. And believe it or not, it shows when one believes in oneself. To be specific, when students believe in themselves, it will show in their appearance. He or she will have confidence, and it will show in how they express certainty.

Have you heard the saying "You never get a second chance to make a first impression?" This statement has truth to it, especially on how one presents himself or herself to the world. How you look and present yourself has a lasting effect on people.

Even if you don't agree 100 percent, you'll at least have to concur that a person's appearance speaks volumes. Therefore, when you present yourself before the world, be mindful of your attire. And yes, I know that these are the years that students want to indulge in self-expression—but, men, you shouldn't appear before others with sagging pants. Is putting on a belt really that much to ask? And, women, you don't have to reveal everything. In other words, don't wear attires that are too tight, too short, or too revealing.

Students should present themselves in the best professional manner, whether through attire or appearance. Remember, first impressions go a long way.

Another level of self-efficiency that leads to professionalism is student confidence. Having a level of poise creates leaders. This is why student confidence has a lot to do with success. Students have to believe in themselves and know that he or she can do whatever they put their minds to. From this point of view, self-confidence is one of the stepping stones that lead to college success.

"The amount of self-confidence a student possesses will affect every aspect of his or her educational goals" ("Self-Confidence and Self-Esteem," 2012). In addition, the article says "when student self-confidence suffers, a student may give up on his or her hopes, dreams, and plans; they may feel unworthy of obtaining their goals or think it is impossible to achieve them."

You must have confidence in your ability to achieve in the face of adversity. This confidence will help one academically, socially, and physically.

How often do you complete only 90 percent of a task? There are times when you will need a capacity to dig deep within to *push* through to complete tasks when every aspect of your being is telling you to quit. You need to have an air of certainty about yourself that says to the world, "I never quit."

Therefore, learn to express certainty through willpower. Students must, in other words, have a personal will to succeed. You cannot have an "I might" or an "I'm going to" mentality. This frame of mind conveys doubt. Maintaining self-efficacy is having a strong *will* that's backed up with pure determination. It's not only having an ability to make things happen but also having an ability to see them through.

Do you have the self-confidence needed to get the job done? Be honest and ask yourself right now, *Of the last ten things I attempted, did I see them all the way through?* If we're really honest with ourselves, most of us can do better in improving our willpower and seeing tasks all the way through. If this is you too, use college as a practice field as you learn to master finishing whatever you start. Over time, this will help you develop a confidence that will lend you a hand in going a long way.

How do we improve our willpower status? I thought you'd never ask! When you've done all that you can do, you must learn to depend on a higher power—a power that has the ability to provide an infinite amount of energy and solutions. Believing in oneself is important, but believing in a power greater than you is even more important because there are many obstacles and pitfalls that await you.

For this reason, learn to connect with your higher power no matter if it's done through meditation or prayer. Just know that you are created to be a confident being and that there is a source that's always willing to revitalize you when you are in need of a little self-assurance.

In Other Words:

Most of the time, bad grades are the results of poor habits. I knew early on that I would have to force myself to change my study habits if I wanted to succeed."

—*Carlyle Edwards,*
University of Tennessee Knoxville

Receiving good grades always validated the hard work and late-night study sessions that I pressed through.

—*Stacey Williams,*
Western Kentucky University

Motivation for me was achieving what others said I would never be able to do.

—*Dr. Sabrina Porcher-Fennell,*
Claflin University

6

Relationships

No man is wise enough by himself.

—*Titus Plautus (250 BC)*

All of us are enclosed in a variety of circles; no matter if it's family, friends, or professional relationships, it's a blessing to be surrounded by a community of people who care for us. Fortunately, we cannot escape being in relationships with others since we are created to be communal creatures. This means that we need each other. Moreover, relationships help us learn a sense of collaboration through our capacity to trust in each other. This is why creating bonds, "both academically and socially," is key to success in college (Gearon, 2015).

Consider this: learning to trust is essential on the academic journey that you are about to embark upon. Therefore, students enrolling into any university need to be mindful of the interactions he or she attempts to obligate themselves to.

As you begin to meet new people, make certain that you surround yourself with people who share similar interests. Maybe you have heard the saying "Birds of a feather flock together." This means that similar people tend to associate with each other, but what about you? Are the people you hang around representative of who you are trying to become? If not, you need to surround yourself with better company.

Make sure that you choose your friends wisely. Be known for keeping the company of other students who progressively take their academic endeavors as serious as you do. The "keeping good company" principle doesn't just apply for academics. It is important that you strive to build healthy relationships in all aspects of your life. No matter if you're in the library, the gym, at work, or at church, always be mindful of this principle.

The reason is simple; you want to lean on people who are a reflection of you. This way, when you need help in any area of your life, you have built a circle of people around you who are willing and able to fill in the gap for you. This is especially true for relatives, peers, and professional associates.

Think about families, for example. A student's family plays an important role in a student's college career because each person's family is vested in seeing him or her succeed. To the best of their ability, your family will be there for you and provide assistance when needed.

As stated earlier, my major was very demanding. I, oftentimes, found myself up during the late hours of the night studying. I was fortunate to have a family who was willing to go the extra mile to see me succeed. They helped greatly by providing childcare assistance for me.

Though I was a young mother attending college, they stood in the gap for me! They would attend to my young child while I read, studied, and even when I needed rest.

Families will assist where they can. Yet students must do their part too because relationships are a two-way street. Make sure that you keep your relatives updated with your college experiences, good or bad. This means that you must reach out to them as well. And there are many ways. I don't care if you send snail mail, text them, e-mail them, or call them. Whatever you do, don't avoid them! Make sure you keep them updated on how college is treating you. Other than that, how else will they know how to help you? Simply put, just put forth an effort to ensure that a strong bond between you and your family members grow.

Building relationships among peers is also an essential part of the college experience. Establishing healthy friendships is important because peers tend to be influential. Since peers can have an effect over people that they are connected to, incoming freshmen should set personal goals to meet people who will encourage them as well as provide support during the initial years of college.

It is no secret that many peer relations are formed during your college years. However, the trick is to connect with people who know how to build you up when life knocks you down. The power of encouragement will help you get back up after your Introduction to Political Science professor shoots down the presentation that you worked on all week.

Everyone needs encouragement, especially in college because it always seems to get a little harder. Think of your friends now. Are they funny or unique? Or is it that you've known them forever? If so, that's good, but do they encourage you? If not, make sure that your upcoming friends are optimistic about encouraging you.

Trust me, these are the types of people you will need during this next phase of your life. Some of the relationships that I developed during my college years are still intact to this day. Most of the relationships that I formed during college didn't last, but there are a few that did. The relationships that lasted were built on the power of support.

Now if you can see that people cling to those that support their dreams and aspirations, be supportive of those who dare to call you a friend. This means that you must also support them when or if they are embarrassed.

For example, if a friend is uncomfortable because of a lack of transportation but has a need to go and get necessities, make it a priority to let your friend know when you are headed toward a supermarket. Your ability to help will encourage your peers to know that they are cared for. Such a simple act of encouragement goes a long way.

Also, when a friend fails, be the first to make it known that they aren't the first to fail, and let them know that they won't be the last. Give them examples of how you've been there, and let them know that getting back up is always the best choice for those who want to succeed.

Evan Esar (1995) said it best when he said, "Failure is not falling down—it is remaining there when you have fallen" (p. 291). To the best of your ability, be supportive by helping your friends get back on their feet. The more you do this, the more friendships you will develop, which should last well beyond your college years.

In addition to relationships with relatives and positive peers, interactions with professional associates such as professors are also necessary. Professor-student relationships are vital to success. They are there to see you flourish.

Professors can help students during office hours. They can point out growth opportunities, and professors can set high expectations for students. Visiting a professor's office is something that most of us did not do in high school. In fact, because of the structure of a teacher's day, most high school teachers don't have office hours set aside for student-teacher interaction. Making time to go to your professor's office is beneficial because he/she can help you with assignments one-on-one. Also, during these office hours, professors can personally get to know you.

Allowing your professor to become familiar with you and vice versa is important. He or she can become familiar with your performance, study, work habits, and can point out growth opportunities. This relationship is also helpful to students when "life" happens. If a student finds himself or herself in a catastrophic situation, professors are willing to be more understanding when the student has gone out of his or her way to develop a relationship with them. So figure out when your professor's office hours are, especially for the tough classes and tough situations that you will encounter during the semester, and quickly schedule times to meet with them.

Another advantage for having a relationship with your professor is that they can become references for future internships and/or graduate programs. When there is a professor-student relationship, the professor will quickly figure out if you have a genuine interest for what is being taught. This will pay off in the future because a reference from a professor holds the weight you'll need to gain acceptance into that special internship or masters program that you have your eye on. Students who have built a rapport with their professors have an advantage because the professors are able to truly speak about the student as a scholar, of the student's character and personal growth.

Professors can also set high expectations for students. Think about it. They are witnessing your growth; therefore, they are in the perfect position to push you to reach heights you never expected. For example, a professor can broaden your perspective by encouraging you to work on projects that he/she knows that you have an interest in. Even if the project is small, such as becoming a research assistant, it will help you see that there is much more to something than what you previously thought. A professor can also expect nothing less than an A from you. For some reason, we fight to obtain a high mark when someone such as a professor believes in us. Get to know your professors and see what he/she can pull out of you.

Professors, peers, and families are there to help you succeed. You must trust, not only in them for guidance, but also in yourself to make the right choices as to whom you let in your relational circles. So select relationships that will mold you into a successful student.

Many relationships are only there for a season, and each relationship has its purpose. A relationship may be in place to show, teach, or tell you something. According to Neill (2014), all of this is essential to our being able to connect successfully with others as adults. It is important that relationships are developed in order to be productive adults in society.

So go forth and choose wisely.

In Other Words

Reestablish yourself in college and do not be afraid to put bad company in the rearview mirror. You will be driven to succeeded or dragged into failure based on the company you keep.

—*Evan Giovanello*, Emory University

Negative relationships add to the stress that college presents. A strong support system and healthy relationships will make college much more fun and enjoyable.

—*Yonathan Nigatu*, Meharry Medical College

Networking with the right people will open doors for you in the future.

—*Terry Bean*, Western Kentucky University

Everyone has a skill; you never know who you may need to help you on your journey.

—*Byron Hall*, Howard University

In my experience, relationships can do more than anything so the old saying is still true; sometimes it is not what you know, but who you know.

—*Elijah D. Holt*, Tennessee State University

7
Positive Mentors

Mentorship is essential. Anyone transitioning from one thing to another definitely needs guidance. To be specific, a mentor is what you will need as you evolve from a high school student to becoming an undergraduate scholar. According to Dictionary.com, a mentor is a wise and trusted counselor. Throughout your college years, you will need someone to steer you during your journey. As you cross over from high school, you will need a mentor to provide advice, counsel, and motivation.

If you do not currently have a mentor, do not worry; just know that there are many places to find positive people who would love to pour into your life such as churches and organizations. Mentors can also be found through community interest groups. When you find someone within any of these associations, they will provide guidance or direction toward your academic and professional accomplishments through modeling and coaching.

As illustrated (on the previous page), mentors wear many hats when it comes to their role of advising students on the unfamiliar, but a mentor's main role is to provide advice. Because each mentor is experienced in their area of expertise, it is important that you obtain mentors that line up with what you enjoy both academically and socially so they can hold you accountable and can share with you in the areas in which they are already familiar with. This is how they will become your inspiration.

Mentors will also counsel you through your program of study, especially if they have experience in that particular area. They will give you options on which direction to take but allow you to think through what needs to be done. Ultimately, you must make the final decisions regarding your academic career. However, when you are unsure of which direction to take, a good mentor will become a personal strategist for you. Your mentor is perfect for these situations because he or she has successfully walked the road you are attempting to stroll down on.

While giving advice and counsel are important aspects of the job, a positive mentor should also be able to provide motivation. In other words, your mentor should inspire you. For example, after guiding you toward obtaining a degree, a great mentor will, in turn, motivate you to do even more—such as to study to enter graduate school or to create a business plan to pursue entrepreneurship. Mentors, for the most part, have years of experience over you, so they should be able to pour enthusiasm into you and your dreams by being an encouraging motivator.

Not only are positive mentors motivators, but they should also be positive role models who demonstrate a character of excellence. Role models illustrate a lifestyle of endurance and represent truth. Patterning after a person of greatness should create a desire for you to follow in their footsteps. Many times, students do not pay attention to individuals who provide advice, counsel, and motivation. Find a role model who will demonstrate success for you to emulate. Role models that represent a positive attitude and behavior are the ones who you should pay close attention to.

By now, you should know that it is very important during your college years to become familiar with a person whom you would like to model after. In addition to advice, counsel, and motivation make sure that your mentor is a good model and can effectively coach you through circumstances that await you.

Does your potential mentor exhibit a character of quality? Do they have an upright demeanor or a vibrant style? Look for these (and many more) qualities in your mentor; they will take you far. A person who carries themselves professionally is one whose charter you should want to pursue. According to Dr. Myles Munroe (2014), the English word *character* comes from a

Latin word meaning "mark" or "distinctive quality." When we talk about one's character, we are talking about a person who will not compromise his or her standards. Again, this raises a few critical questions: what is your perspective mentor's personality like? Does your potential mentor's personality express an appeasing temperament? Does he or she remain calm in hostile situations? Can he or she keep a professional disposition? You must ask yourself these types of questions because the idea is to surround yourself with a person who will always[10] display a positive outlook.

Another quality that a good role model should have is a positive demeanor. Remember, students, your demeanor goes a long way, so you want to be associated with a person who exemplifies the same positive manner. Students, you need to know how a person's demeanor is

---

[10] At least to the best of their ability because we must also be cognitive of the fact that no one is perfect.

foreseen outwardly. In other words, are they who they say they are? You do not want to be associated with a person who exemplifies a false personality.

In addition to demeanor, positive role models should have a style about them. These individuals are classy in their own way. They carry themselves skillfully, gracefully, and they are very knowledgeable in their area of expertise. You want to seek a role model who is able to impart knowledge upon you and leave you with ideas you never thought of. Make sure that your role model's style is impressionable and makes you better than before you became his or her mentee.

Besides making sure that your mentor can model well before you, make sure that he or she also has the skills to coach you through the many obstacles that will try to stand in your way on your journey toward success. Yes, positive mentors should also be able to coach individuals.

An academic coach is one who teaches "learning strategies and life management skills" (the University of Tennessee, Knoxville: The Student Success Center, 2014).

Your coach/mentor will help you develop appropriate learning strategies. A coach will train individuals through the process headed toward victory. For instance, coaches will teach students how to be effective note takers or rapid readers. This is beneficial for all majors especially health, business, and science. Yet individuals must want to be taught in order for coaches to personalize each student's academic success plan. It is important for students to meet with their mentoring coach at the beginning, middle, and end of each semester. Make it a priority; add it to your semester planner. A personalized plan will keep you focused through the year.

A mentor/coach also teaches life management skills. Two things that you should hope to gain advice on from your coach are (1) money management and (2) what it takes to remain safe/healthy. Though these lessons are not new ideas, being reminded of the importance of these areas in college is where your mentor/coach can play an important role in your success.

Your mentor/coach is there to remind you about the importance of managing your money and the importance of not accumulating debt. "The decisions that you make on a daily basis, or monthly or even a one-time expense all factors into your larger experience" (Boyington, 2014). Money can slip away so easy. This is why a mentoring coach can enlighten you on how to maintain a budget, paying your bills, and why you should avoid receiving credit cards so early because "student loan debt will affect your quality of life after graduation" (Boyington, 2014).

One other life-managing skill your mentoring coach can help you with is staying safe. Staying safe and healthy is especially important when you are introduced to a new environment. For example, students have to be aware of their surroundings and know to never walk across campus alone in the dark. A coach can also tell you of the importance of going out in groups. This method better ensures your safety. Your mentoring coach will enlighten you on these conversations (and many more) with you for safety purposes.

This last point may seem obvious, but managing your nutrition is vital to remaining healthy. In college, you may not be able to run home for meals as much as you would like. Many students who reside on campus have a meal plan attached to their tuition. This ensures daily meals. But these meal allotments can disappear before a semester closes out. With life-managing skills your mentor/coach can teach you how to stretch your meal plan out over the semester and why you should cook more often. Cooking will help you not have to run to the cafeteria every time you are hungry. This will also help you use your meal plan less frequently to ensure that it lasts the whole semester. Besides, cooking amongst your peers is a way of bonding and getting to know individuals in your dorm. These are some of the life-management strategies your mentor/coach should be able to share with you to help make your transition from high school as smooth as possible.

Having a positive mentor/coach, adds to the support required to truly succeed. Make sure that your mentor can effectively coach you through the unfamiliar world that lies ahead, can give good advice, counsel, and are able to keep you motivated. Spend enough time with them to ensure that they can pass on the learning strategies and life-management skills you'll need to become successful students.

In Other Words

Seeing someone thrive in what you hope to do in your future provides inspiration, hope, and motivation. Knowing what steps to take and which pitfalls to avoid will help in the success of your future.

—*Stacey Williams,*
Western Kentucky University

Freshmen need people who can guide them through the highs and lows of their first and second semesters.

—*Miranda Jones*
American Baptist College

Role models provide true lifelong friendships, business relationships, life coaching, guidance, and future references.

—*Theron Blair,*
Middle Tennessee State University

8
Resources

You may be asking the question, "Why are resources important?" Or better yet, "What are resources?" According to Dictionary.com, a resource is a source of supply, support, or aid, especially one that can be readily drawn upon when needed. Simply put, for most, resources can be a "help button."

Yes, a help button (or resources) is especially important for students. In particular, students enrolled from other states are often unfamiliar with the area and must find where help is provided quickly. It's not just out-of-towners; most students are unaware that there are many resources they can use to simplify potential catastrophes. Become familiar with area agencies, stores, organizations, pharmacies, etc., to assist in particular areas of need. No matter if it's an academic, emotional, social, or physical dilemma, students should be aware that there are resources available to help them work through almost all issues.

When students don't maintain a clear head and relaxed state, they will struggle academically. Academic services can assist with this problem. These services can support students in many ways.

For one, academic resources can help students stay abreast of their studies through tutoring services. Tutoring sessions are set up to strengthen you in areas or courses that you may find difficult. Almost all departments have labs that can enhance your academic dilemmas. If you are willing to spend a few extra hours in some labs, you will be surprised how such a simple resource can make a big difference.

Another resource important to familiarize yourself with is agencies that deal with your emotional aspect. It is important for students to be able to talk to someone when the need is there. The resource that assists with your emotional being is the counseling center. At most colleges, counseling services can be obtained on campus. On other instances, counseling services are off campus but can still easily be found with today's technology.

Besides, counseling can provide an opportunity for students to talk or sort out thoughts. It can also help students get through unbearable crises. Therefore, students should know where to seek help, whether on or off campus.

Check your website or contact a mentor. Whatever you do, make sure you take advantage of counseling services. It is important that you keep a sound mind because it will also help you move closer toward your success. There will be times when you may feel overwhelmed or even stressed out, but you should know where to go to deal with these emotions. Do not be ashamed either. This is the purpose for a counseling center—to help you work through your emotions. When students do not address their emotions, it will interfere with their learning. Learning is derived from attention—which, in turn, drives memory and knowledge ("How Emotions Affect Learning," 1994). Students should take advantage of counseling services as needed to ensure that class attention is maintained and that learning remains a continuous process.

Oftentimes, students become so bogged down with study and assignments that they forget to take care of themselves. Becoming familiar with agencies where you can get help with assignments, attending support groups to talk, or being familiar with a massage therapist to relax are essential to remaining a balanced student. These resources are ones that students should know how to access as needed. My hope is that you do not find these services at the last minute because then it may be too late. Universities have placed these services in place because they understand that the emotional state of students is something that should be taken seriously to ensure students succeed. Because these services are available, please, access when needed.

Another resource that can help students is the social aspect of learning to manage the "college life" that you must steer through with your peers. There are many things that can help you in this area, such as joining campus organizations and involving yourself with study groups.

It is important for students to become familiar with on-campus organizations. On-campus organizations assist students in bonding with other students and having a sense of belonging. When students are involved with on-campus groups, they are more likely to stay enrolled because they have a sense of responsibility to their peers. Students who are involved quickly become somewhat obligated and accountable to others. This is a quality that will outlast your college years.

The student affairs department or student union building is a great place to start to learn about campus organizations. These departments assist students in knowing how to become involved. For example, student government association (SGA), marching band, forensic teams, sororities, or fraternities are great places to plant yourselves in college. These organizations assist students in growing and thriving socially.

Students can research what each of these clubs or campus organizations have to offer. This is where you can bond, grow, and develop a greater understanding of yourself and others. The whole purpose for familiarizing yourself with on-campus groups is so you can get to know positive people at your institution who also want to succeed.

Being part of study groups is another resource that students should learn to take advantage of. Study groups are often developed on or off campus. The purpose for study groups is to help students retain and recall information through synergy. A good study group is often formed around your particular program of study. Students who are in similar programs of study, such as science for example, are more familiar with key concepts and theories as opposed to studying with one whose major is English.

Students in your program of study can be a key component to starting a study group. So it is important for you to get to know other students in each of your classes. Obtain students' contact information from each class. This will help you when questions arise where other peers may have grasped a better understanding than you did on a particular assignment. Organize study sessions well before tests are scheduled. This is where having other peer telephone numbers or e-mail addresses can be a valuable resource.

One last source you should be aware of is how to obtain resources that can help when physical issues arise. Your local pharmacy is always a good place to start. Knowing where each local pharmacy is located and the hours of each is something you should learn within your first or second week of school.

These resources are necessary when you need food, medication, or hygiene products. It will feel good to know in advance where you need to go when the time comes. Having a toothache at 1:00 a.m. or stomach cramps at four in the morning is easily solved when you know that there is a twenty-four-hour Walgreens just up the street. This off-campus resource is essential especially when you need to pick up medication after normal business hours.

Believe it or not, this small piece of information will be a boost of enthusiasm to both your emotional and physical state. It is not only important for local students but also out-of-state students to know where certain resources are located. Students enrolled in colleges or universities are oftentimes not aware of resources in the area, especially if he or she is from another state.

Students should be aware of the resources that can assist them when they need help academically, emotionally, socially, or physically. It is important for you to become familiar with area agencies, stores, organizations, pharmacies, etc., to assist in any particular area. Don't overlook the power of knowing what resources are available.

In Other Words

Not all the time did I find resources when I needed them; however, I would reach out to my professors or mentors for direction.

—Frederick Cartwright Jr.,
Fisk University

Finding proper resources are not always easy, but asking questions and asking the right people is the key to solving any problem.

—Yonathan Nigatu,
Meharry Medical College

Exploring your college website is always a good resource.

—Carlyle Edwards,
University of Tennessee Knoxville

PART III

9

Responsibility

When you take responsibility for yourself, you will develop a hunger to accomplish your dreams.

—*Les Brown*

University students have great times, yet they also have great responsibilities. What a student does during the course of his or her college years is what he or she will be held accountable for in the many years that follow. Understand early what your limits are, and try to stay within those boundaries. Oftentimes, students bite off more than they can chew.

For example, one may agree to a church presentation that is required next week when he or she already has the responsibility of presenting a class project. Students have great intentions when they agree to take on certain assignments on top of the school responsibilities in their life. No matter if it is personal agendas or social events, academics should remain a top responsibility.

Students often feel bad when they are unable to fulfill their obligations or duties. What they fail to realize is that being responsible is all about having an ability to prioritize. Students who are responsible understand the importance of being assertive; being mindful of university routines, homework assignments, and grades; and being independent.

In order for students to have college success, he or she must play their part by stepping up. Sheryl Sandberg asks a critical question in her book, *Lean In*. She asks, "What would you do if you weren't scared?" In other words, you must make it your responsibility to be assertive. Here is the reason: confident students are able to tackle insecurities, which over time spill over into their academic and social life.

According to Mueller (2011), "students who have self-confidence take responsibility for him or herself and others, trusts in his or her abilities, face his or her fears, and expand their own boundaries, scrutinize criticism, and do not blame others for his or her own mistakes." Assertive students are those who know where they stand, and they take great accountability in all that is said and done.

Do you take responsibility for your actions? Taking responsibility or being mindful of one's own abilities is a forward-thinking process. Students must be aware of the outcomes of their actions. If you can live with this, then learn to be assertive because confident people, over time, always become leaders.

Being mindful of university course routines is another way one can be responsible. There is a big difference between high school and university course requirements. In other words, it is your responsibility to choose classes that are beneficial to your college success. High school class requirements are more dependent where college class requirements are more independent. Dependent meaning students rely on teachers, parents, and the school's curriculum to move them forward. On the contrary, independent means that you carve out your own direction as long as you stay within the confines of your major.

Do know that you are assigned an academic advisor to help you through this transition. An academic advisor will help you become a more independent student. They will assist you in choosing your college courses at the outset. Eventually, you will not need assistance from your academic advisor as you will initially.

Nonetheless, are you aware of your current advisor? What are his or her office hours? It is your responsibility to make sure your academic advisor knows who you are.

Third, in college, it is the responsibility of students to complete assignments and turn them in on time. It is not the responsibility of teachers, professors, or parents to remind students of their homework assignments as was the case so often in high school. Yes, in high school, many of us were accustomed to being reminded several times when assignments and projects were due or needed to be turned in. In contrast, college is very different. Professors will assign work and expect each student to get it turned in as scheduled.

At the beginning of each class, professors will provide each student with a syllabus that provides detailed information of objectives, expectations, and requirements for the class. Homework assignments and readings are addressed in each student's syllabus. Sometimes, homework assignments may not be graded or taken up, but you may still be required to know the material if called upon. Again, this is the difference between dependent and independent learning.

For the most part, high school students seldom read or review notes outside of class and, oftentimes, only spend zero to two hours outside of class studying. Outside-of-class study for college students is required for greater understanding and requires at least two to three hours of study ("How Is College Different from High School," 2014).

Therefore, it is the responsibility of each student to take advantage of independent time for college success. In other words, stay up on your homework assignments by studying and reading during your downtime. This will help you stand out, especially during your transition from high school to college. Developing a strong sense of being responsible with your assignments should translate to good grades.

Grades are a major component that indicates college success. Throughout your college experience, students must maintain a certain grade point average (GPA). One's grade point average determines one's success ("Diversity and Democracy: Civic Learning for Shared Future," 2014). Your grade point average sets you apart from your peers for employment recognition as you begin to interview for certain positions.

Now I know that you know that students pass their classes when they meet departmental requirements, and I also believe that you know that each class passed cumulates into a grade point average. However, as it pertains to GPAs, I definitely want you to know that staying mindful of your grade percentage will assist you in the future. I say this because you need to know from the onset that people, companies, and graduate programs will judge you based on your GPA. With that being said, give them something good to look at. Set yourself up from the beginning to maintain a high GPA, especially since you know that people are judging you because of a number (GPA).

The last key to becoming responsible is ensuring that you strive to become independent. After enrolling into your choice institution, make it a point to learn self-governing skills. As stated earlier, during students' high school years, students are very dependent. This suggests that teachers, for the most part, provide reminders for their students. Learn quicker than later that you must become more proactive and responsible.

For example, if you are struggling with a class, it is your responsibility to seek out your professor's assistance. Make it a point to visit him or her during set office hours. Do not hope that they will pull you aside and ask if you need help (though if they do, that would be nice). To ensure college success, play an active role in your own achievements by recognizing that you must strive for independence.

Believe me, college has a special way of making students grow up fast. If you fail to learn this lesson, I'm not sure if you will be able to hang around any campus long because most universities have a funny way of dealing with students who fail to step up and be independent.

In order for students to have college success, he or she must play their part by being responsible! It is important for students to understand what their responsibilities are: be assertive, stay mindful of university course routines, take homework assignments seriously, do what it takes to maintain GPA, and strive to become independent. Growing into a responsible student is important to understand because no one will be held for their actions but them. Remind yourself daily that you are depending on yourself.

In Other Words

Go to class; all the time. Take good notes; turn your notes into study sheets prior to tests because 80 percent of test material is covered in class. Note: this did not work for me in Math and Spanish.

—*Evan Giovanello,*
Emory University

When it comes to studying, PROCRASTINATION is the enemy! Just get it over with.

—*Dominique Burkes,*
University of Tennessee Chattanooga

This may go against conventional wisdom, but get plenty of rest because a rested mind is a focused mind.

—*Michael Harris,*
Jackson State University

Rushing through a study session is definitely a hindrance, so give yourself plenty of time to study before a test.

—*Stacey Williams,*
Western Kentucky University

10

Expectations

High expectation is the key to everything.

—Sam Walton

No matter where you find yourself, there will always be expectations to adhere to. In our case, students must understand the expectations of universities. All institutions have high expectations for incoming students. They are often put in place in order for students to have college success.

For students to have college success there are things expected from learners. For example, students must attend classes regularly and on time, remain honest academically, and follow codes of conduct. These expectations are not only put in place so students can be successful, but also to keep students accountable and safe. Creating high expectations for students should put students on a path that leads toward success. Since you are elevating your status from high school to college, you should also anticipate needing to raise your level of expectations to flourish.

Fortunately, attending classes regularly and on time was not a problem for me in college. While attending the state university, I was not one to hang out at parties or hang out late nights. This allowed me to attend classes regularly and on time. I understood the importance of what it took to complete and pass a class or course. I would suggest to those who do choose to party to *not* hang out late on the nights that you have early morning classes the next day.

Attending class on time is important, but coming regularly is just as important too. To fully grasp the material that instructors hope one learns, students must make it customary to show up to class. Students must be mindful of what he or she hopes to gain in the long term—a degree. To obtain a degree though, one must achieve many short-term goals, such as passing each class. In other words, going to many classes is a process that leads to graduating eventually. So, students, take advantage of every learning experience. Fortunately, I was familiar with completing what was required to obtain my degree.

In addition to being on time and going to class, try to fully immerse yourself in the material. Write thought-provoking papers, ask tough questions, and wow your peers with remarkable presentations. Do not just go through the motions. If so, you will miss your opportunity to grow as a person by missing what college has to offer, which is the ability to change your perspective. Just going through the motions of barely completing required material does not assist one in gaining from a true learning experience. Students must enroll into institutions expecting to learn and experience growth.

Part of obtaining a learning experience is academic integrity. Academic honesty is important; it shows how much you have learned. Truthfully, when you cheat, you only fool yourself. This is why institutions expect students to maintain high levels of educational integrity. The reason why academic honesty is so important is because it depicts students' character as well as establishes the university's reputation.

Dictionary.com defines *reputation* as "the estimation in which a person or thing is held, especially by the community or the public." In our case, one's reputation generally refers to what others believe, feel, or think about an individual.

As scholars, you are in a unique position to develop your reputation as to how people look at you, good or bad. According to Wenger, McDermott, and Snyder (2002), "successful practice building goes hand in hand with community building." Establishing best practices as it pertains to academic honesty will build a good reputation for institutions and students alike.

For instance, making sure you cite others' quotes is very important. Citing and crediting authors go hand in hand with academic honesty.

What are the rules for citing work at your institution? What are the rules for establishing yourself as one that is trustworthy? Students from any institution should have a clear understanding of what it takes to maintain academic honesty. The process of students practicing academic honesty over time establishes a good reputation.

People with good reputations are often recognized as those who can lead others just because of status alone. The struggle for status becomes a key motivating force (McCabe and Pavela, 2004). This becomes even more evident as graduation draws nearer. Believe me; companies come looking for those of high stature or those who have elevated their status through having an outstanding character.

Each college and university wants to be known as the institution that produces students who demonstrate a reputation of academic honesty. Colleges and universities that require its students to maintain academic honesty will have a reputation for this practice in the community. Also, students who practice academic honesty will carry high esteem in the community based on the college or university's reputation. Both the student and the institution need each other.

To achieve academic honesty, make certain that it is seen throughout your work. Make it a habit to demonstrate integrity; this behavior is important. Students should practice academic honesty inside and outside the classroom. Students enrolled in an academic program should maintain the reputation of the institution and uphold decent principles (Lipson, 2008). This is the expectation of every student enrolled in a college or university. Just remember—when you make integrity a habit, it's a win-win for both you and your institution.

A final expectation that students should be aware of is their institution's code of conduct. When transitioning from high school to college, each student should know what is expected of them. Students should at least have an idea that the college experience will be somewhat different than their high school experience.

One change will be the university's code of conduct. Codes of conduct are rules and regulations that govern individuals. Students' awareness of the institution's code of conduct will keep them safe and in compliance with the institution's expectations. They provide step-by-step directions on what students can and cannot do as it pertains to academics and behavior. This way, there are no excuses for incoming students who think they can get away with this or that.

Most likely, the codes of conduct will cover all aspects to ensure that the institution is not held liable for the crazy things students think they can get away with. Also, the rules are created to make certain that the students are privileged to be in an environment conducive for quality learning. So, in essence, the code of conduct provides awareness. Students must always make themselves aware of the university's expectations, policies, and procedures.

These new expectations provide students a new way to blossom on a higher plain. For example, each class provides a syllabus of what to look forward to for the class and explains course of actions for pertinent questions. The syllabus shares information about the teacher, tardiness of papers, assignments, and grading information. This information is important to keep students aware of procedures and help maintain academic success.

When enrolling in a college/university institution, students are expected to sign a code of conduct agreement. Most agreements include rules that regulate activities or affairs such as the following:

Academic honesty, alcohol, complicity, disruptive conduct, illegal drugs, endangering the safety of others, fire safety, unsuitable guests, hazing, misuse of services or property, residence hall regulations, responsible computing and use of university computer resources, sexual assault, discriminatory harassment, stalking, how to govern yourselves within student organizations, theft, violence, weapons, etc.

This agreement suggests that each student will abide by the codes of conduct within the university. Students maintaining the codes of conduct heighten the university's reputation throughout the community at large. It is important for students to understand early that abusing the code of conduct has serious consequences attached.

Therefore, if you are not aware of the institution's expectations, take a moment to reflect on them. If they are not found easily, ask your academic advisor, or maybe your mentor can point you in the right direction of finding them. The point is to make sure that you not only sign them but are aware of what you have signed your name to. The reason for this is so that you know the importance of maintaining academic honesty, conduct, and behavior. In addition, you are also aware of the consequences when you do not comply.

Do not fear. The university wants you to succeed. That is why the rules exist. So as you go forward, follow the rules and regulations of your institution to ensure the community's safety. As you do, watch how a level of excellence quickly becomes your new normal.

Knowing what's expected of you is not just a college normalcy. With everything you do, there is an expectation. When you become gainfully employed, they will have expectations for you as well. Being successful in college will prepare you for the next phase of life.

People are held to levels of expectation; so always expect more of yourself, and you will always get more in return. This also goes for your university. Whatever your expectation is of your institution, make sure those expectations guide you toward a successful life.

In Other Words

I expected more of myself academically when I went to college because it was more challenging and costly.

—*Kosher Brilly,*
Fisk University

My level of expectations changed after I realized the importance and seriousness of knowing the information in my field of study. Mastering that information was truly life changing.

—*Frederick Cartwright Jr.,*
Fisk University

I expected more of myself, especially after understanding what the real world would offer me upon graduation.

—*Antonio Marks,*
Tennessee State University

Students, as I close, I expect you to go forth and conquer. As you transition, make sure to become all you can be!

For speaking engagements or to inform me of success stories, please contact me via e-mail:

makingthejump1@gmail.com

Notes:

Notes:

References

Adams, C. 2010. "Most Students Aren't Ready for College, ACT Data Show." Retrieved from http://hechingerreport.org/content/most-students-arent-ready-for-college-act-data-show_12951/.

Beyond the Rhetoric." 2010. Retrieved from http://www.highereducation.org/reports/college_readiness/gap.shtml.

Diversity and Democracy: Civic Learning for Shared Future." 2014. Retrieved from http://www.diversityweb.org/DiversityDemocracy/vol13no3/report.cfm.

Esar, E. 1995. *20,000 Quips and Quotes: A Treasury of Witty Remarks, Comic Proverbs, Wisecracks, and Epigrams.* New York: Barnes & Noble Books.

Hearon, C. 2015. "Your Goal: Four Fabulous Years. Best Colleges": *U.S. News and World Report,* p. 14.

How Is College Different from High School?" 2014. Retrieved from http://www.smu.edu/Provost/ALEC/NeatStuffforNewStudents/HowIsCollegeDifferentfromHighSchool.

Hyman, J., and Jacobs, L. 2010. "10 Reasons to Go to a Small College." *U.S. News and World Report.* Retrieved from http://www.usnews.com/education/blogs /professors-guide/2010/07/28/10-reasons-to-go-to-a-small-college.

Keller, G. 2004. *Transforming a College: A Story of a Little-Known College's Strategic Climb to National Distinction.* Baltimore, Maryland: Johns Hopkins University Press.

Long, B. T. 2009. "Usable Knowledge (2009)." Retrieved from http://www.uknow.gse.harvard.edu/leadership/LP101-407.html.

Mueller, S. 2011. "Building Self-Confidence." Retrieved from http://www.planetofsuccess.com/selfconfidence.

Munroe, M. 2014. *The Power of Character in Leadership: How Values, Morals, Ethics, and Principles Affect Leaders.* New Kensington, Pennsylvania: Whitaker House.

Neill, Dr. N. 2014. "What Is the Purpose of Relationships?" Retrieved from http://www.neillneill.com/what-is-the-purpose-of-relationships.

Rivers, S. 2014. "Extracurricular Activities and Academic Grades." Retrieved from http://classroom.synonym.com/extracurricular-activities-academic-grades-4906.html.

Sandberg, S. 2013. *Lean In: Women, Work, and the Will to Lead.* New York, New York: Alfred A. Knopf Press.

"Self-Confidence and Self-Esteem." 2012. Retrieved from http://www.edu-nova.com/articles/student-confidence.

Strike, A. 2014. "The Benefits of Stress." Retrieved from http://psychcentral.com/blog/archives/2014/04/15/the-benefits-of-stress.

"Surviving College." 2014. Retrieved from http://www.umflint.edu/advising/surviving_college.

"The University of Tennessee Knoxville: The Student Success Center." 2014. Retrieved from http://studentsuccess.utk.edu/support/coaches.

Index

A

academic honesty, 122–28
academics, 74, 110, 126
airline school, 12, 14
American College Test (ACT), 11, 15–16, 25
assignments, 42–47, 66, 80, 100, 110, 114–17, 127

B

behavior, 28, 56, 89, 125–28,

C

career, 13, 15, 23–24
challenges, 14, 54–56, 58, 60
clubs, 47, 102
codes of conduct, 119, 125–28
college, 11–12, 15, 17–19, 22, 24–28, 30, 35, 37–43, 45–
    50, 54–56, 58-61, 65-68, 70, 73, 75–79, 85, 89, 93–
    94, 99, 101-05, 109–17, 119–25, 127–29
college experiences, 24, 36, 62, 79, 118, 129
college success, 17, 27–28, 45, 50, 65, 68, 110–17, 119
conflict management, 54, 60
coping skills, 18, 53, 55–61
counseling services, 99–101

D

degree, 23, 32, 88, 121

E

emotions, 56, 100
exercising, 41, 44, 48, 51, 54, 59
expectations, 17-18, 79-81, 113, 119-20, 126-29
extracurricular activities, 25, 47–49, 51

O

on-campus groups, 101–03
organizations, 31, 33–36, 47, 51, 86, 101–05, 128

P

peers, 43, 75–79, 82, 95, 101–03, 115, 121
prioritize, 42, 44, 47, 110
procrastination, 41, 49, 118
professors, 27, 43, 79–82, 113
professor-student relationships, 79, 81

R

reading, 18, 23, 27, 33, 45, 54, 58, 113–4
relationships, 60, 73–83
reputation, 122–25, 128
requirements, 13, 46, 55, 111–15
resources, 97–98, 100, 104–5, 128
responsibility, 14, 46, 102, 109–16
role models, 88–91

S

Sandberg, Sheryl, 110
Scholastic Aptitude Test (SAT), 11, 15–16
self-confidence, 68–70, 111
self-efficacy, 65–66, 69
self-efficiency, 65, 68
self-expression, 67
social events, 42–43, 110
social life, 48, 110
status, 70, 120, 124
stewardess, 12–14
stress, 57–60, 100
student affairs department, 102
student government association (SGA), 102
students, 16–18, 22, 24–27, 32–38, 43, 45–50, 54–58, 60,
    65–69, 74, 76, 79–81, 87–88, 90, 92, 94–95, 97–3,
    105, 109, 110–17, 119–28

student union. *See* student affairs department

study groups, 45, 101, 103

T

time management, 41–43, 48–50, 55

transition, 15, 17–19, 32, 66, 85, 95, 112, 114, 125

U

university, 11, 15–16, 18, 24, 26, 33–34, 38, 45, 47, 49, 51, 59, 74, 92, 109–11, 117, 122, 124–29

V

vision, 17–18, 21–26, 28–29, 32, 34, 36

W

willpower, 65, 69–70

CPSIA information can be obtained
at www.ICGtesting.com
Printed in the USA
LVOW01s1434280217
525681LV00006B/33/P